G000077389

This edition copyright © 2002 Lion Publishing
Illustrations copyright © 2002 Jane Tattersfield

Published by
Lion Publishing plc
Mayfield House, 256 Banbury Road,
Oxford OX2 7DH, England
www.lion-publishing.co.uk
ISBN 0 7459 4641 0

First edition 2002
1 3 5 7 9 10 8 6 4 2 0

Music acknowledgments

℗ 2002 Classic Fox Records
Recording under licence from Classic Fox Records UK
www.foxrecords.co.uk

Text acknowledgments

Scriptures are quoted from the Good News Bible
published by The Bible Societies/HarperCollins
Publishers Ltd, UK © American Bible Society
1966, 1971, 1976, 1992, used with permission.

Every effort has been made to trace and acknowledge
copyright holders of all the quotations in this book.
We apologize for any errors or omissions that may
remain, and would ask those concerned to contact the
publishers, who will ensure that full acknowledgment
is made in the future.

A catalogue record for this book is available
from the British Library

Typeset in Lapidary 333
Printed and bound in Singapore

The Spirit of Christmas

Illustrated by Jane Tattersfield

LION
Giftlines

The Angels

*An angel of the Lord appeared to them, and the
glory of the Lord shone over them. They were terribly
afraid, but the angel said to them,*

*'Don't be afraid! I am here with good news
for you, which will bring great joy to all the people.
This very day in David's town your Saviour was born
– Christ the Lord! And this is what will prove it to
you: you will find a baby wrapped in strips of cloth
and lying in a manger.'*

*Suddenly a great army of heaven's angels appeared
with the angel, singing praises to God:*

*'Glory to God in the highest heaven, and peace
on earth to those with whom he is pleased!'*

From the Gospel of Luke, chapter 2

We all speak the language of peace and joy at Christmas-time, and yet these things can be hard to find or to put into practice. Holiday fun and entertainment, a break from work and spending time with loved ones are all wonderful things, and yet they can bring with them busyness, anxiety, frustration, or bitter-sweet memories of previous years.

Consider the figures of the angels.

They remind us of that first Christmas and its significance.

They encourage us that there can be purpose and direction in our lives today.

They challenge us to put aside the non-essentials and focus on what is really important.

They call us to be joyful.

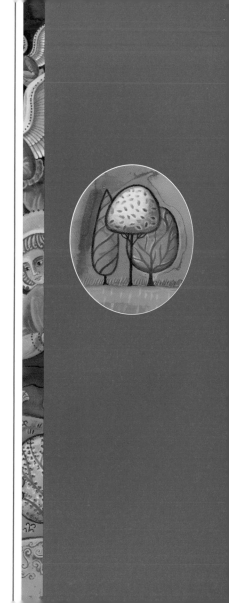

The angel of the Lord came down
And glory shone around.

Nahum Tate

O, a voice from the sky, Lady,
It seemed to us then,
Telling of God being born
In the world of men.

Author unknown

I will honour Christmas in my heart,
and try to keep it all the year.

Charles Dickens

As children we had a sense of wonder. Our eyes were wide open and drinking in the fascinating gifts we beheld. Our thirsty souls could not have enough of the wonders of creation. Then, somehow, we grew too old to dream. We tired of the abundance of the world, or at least grew weary of keeping up with the feast of life, and stepped away from the banquet of life.

Author unknown

Ding dong! merrily on high,
In heaven the bells are ringing:
Ding dong! verily the sky
Is riven with angels singing.
Gloria, hosanna in excelsis!

Traditional

The Shepherds

When the angels went away from them back into heaven, the shepherds said to one another, 'Let's go to Bethlehem and see this thing that has happened.'

So they hurried off and found Mary and Joseph and saw the baby lying in the manger. When the shepherds saw him, they told them what the angel had said about the child. All who heard it were amazed at what the shepherds said.

The shepherds went back, singing praises to God for all they had heard and seen; it had been just as the angel had told them.

From the Gospel of Luke, chapter 2

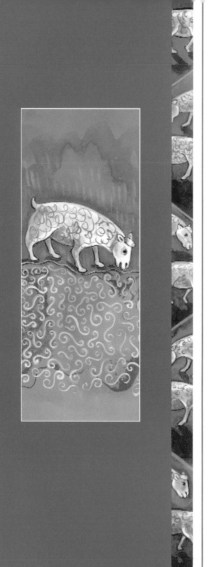

Daily life, for us as for the shepherds on the hills all those centuries ago, can be all-consuming. We are seldom able, at Christmas or at any other time, to stop to look around us. Or when we do, the stresses and strains can be all we see: a jumble of shopping, cooking, travelling and television. It can seem an immense effort to pause even for a moment to think beyond the immediate situation.

Consider the figures of the shepherds.

They remind us to look and listen and act on what we see.

They encourage us to be open to change, to move on and not to be afraid.

They challenge us to take a step outside and beyond the daily routine and to see what surprises lie in store.

They call us to be adventurous.

Silent night, holy night,
Shepherds quake at the sight.
Glories stream from heaven afar,
Heavenly hosts sing alleluia;
Christ the Saviour is born,
Christ the Saviour is born!

Joseph Mohr

What child is this, who, laid to rest,
On Mary's lap is sleeping?
Whom angels greet with anthems sweet,
While shepherds watch are keeping?
This, this is Christ the King,
Whom shepherds guard and angels sing:
Haste, haste to bring him laud,
The babe, the son of Mary.

W.C. Dix

Life is a constant Advent season: we are continually
waiting to become, to discover, to complete, to fulfil.
Hope, struggle, fear, expectation and fulfilment are all
part of our Advent experience.

Author unknown

It is easy to think Christmas,
and it is easy to believe Christmas,
but it is hard to act Christmas.

Author unknown

Take time to be aware that in the very midst of
our busy preparations for the celebration of Christ's
birth in ancient Bethlehem, Christ is reborn in the
Bethlehems of our homes and daily lives. Take time,
slow down, be still…

Edward Hays

The Mother

The angel said to her, 'Don't be afraid, Mary; God has been gracious to you. You will become pregnant and give birth to a son, and you will name him Jesus. He will be great and will be called the Son of the Most High God.'

Mary said to the angel, 'I am a virgin. How, then, can this be?'

The angel answered, 'The Holy Spirit will come on you, and God's power will rest upon you. For this reason the holy child will be called the Son of God. For there is nothing that God cannot do.'

'I am the Lord's servant,' said Mary; 'may it happen to me as you have said.'

From the Gospel of Luke, chapter 1

The media reminds us each Christmas that this is a golden opportunity to spend time with family and friends, perhaps rarely seen throughout the year. And yet the happy smiling families we see on posters and on screen are surely unrealistic. More often, despite, or perhaps because of, the love we bear each other, pressures and tensions can come to the surface, or it seems strangely difficult and risky to express one's deepest hopes and fears.

Consider the figure of the mother.

It reminds us to reach out to others in love.

It encourages us to take the time to nurture our most important relationships.

It challenges us to have faith and patience in all situations.

It calls us to be vulnerable.

*F*or Christ is born of Mary,
And, gathered all above,
While mortals sleep, the angels keep
Their watch of wondering love.

O morning stars, together
Proclaim the holy birth!
And praises sing to God the King,
And peace to men on earth.

Phillips Brooks

*A*nd the mother wondered and
    bowed her head,
And sat as still as a statue of stone.

Henry Wadsworth Longfellow

The Gospel account of the Christmas event is full of activity. And yet, in the middle of the frenetic action, here is this woman wrapped in mystical silence. She demonstrates the necessity of a quiet place within ourselves at Christmas-time – that place where we are most ourselves in relation to God.

William Frebuger

The world is not as just, not as loving, not as whole as we know it can and should be. But the coming of Christ and his presence among us – as one of us – give us reason to live in hope: that light will shatter the darkness, that we can be liberated from our fears and prejudices, that we are never alone or abandoned.

Author unknown

The Kings

Some men came from the east to Jerusalem and asked,
  'Where is the baby born to be the king of the Jews?
We saw his star when it came up in the east, and we
have come to worship him.'

  The star they had seen in the east went ahead of
them until it stopped over the place where the child
was. They went into the house, and when they saw
the child with his mother Mary, they knelt down and
worshipped him. They brought out their gifts of gold,
frankincense and myrrh, and presented them to him.

From the Gospel of Matthew, chapter 2

 $\mathcal{J}$ ust as the three kings brought gifts to the baby Jesus, so we give gifts to those who are special to us. And yet the buying of presents can so easily become a burden, as we rush around worrying that we will not be able to find the 'right' gift, or becoming dizzy with the amount of choice available. It is difficult to slow down and enjoy the experience of giving.

Consider the figures of the kings.

They remind us how to celebrate our relationships through our gifts.

They encourage us to choose wisely and to give as an expression of love.

They challenge us to focus on giving rather than receiving.

They call us to be generous.

I saw three ships come sailing in
On Christmas Day, on Christmas Day.
I saw three ships come sailing in
On Christmas Day in the morning.

And what was in those ships all three
On Christmas Day, on Christmas Day?
And what was in those ships all three
On Christmas Day in the morning?

The Virgin Mary and Christ were there
On Christmas Day, on Christmas Day.
The Virgin Mary and Christ were there
On Christmas Day in the morning.

Traditional

What can I give him,
Poor as I am?

Christina Rossetti

When the song of the angels is stilled,
When the star in the sky is gone,
When the kings and princes are home,
When the shepherds are back with the flocks,
Then the work of Christmas begins:

    to find the lost,

    to heal those broken in spirit,

    to feed the hungry,

    to release the oppressed,

    to rebuild the nations,

    to bring peace among all peoples,

    to make a little music with the heart.

Howard Thurman

Carols

The First Nowell
God Rest Ye Merry, Gentlemen
Ding Dong! Merrily on High
Silent Night
What Child Is This?
O Come, All Ye Faithful
Away in a Manger
O Little Town of Bethlehem
The Holly and the Ivy
I Saw Three Ships
Jingle Bells
Good King Wenceslas